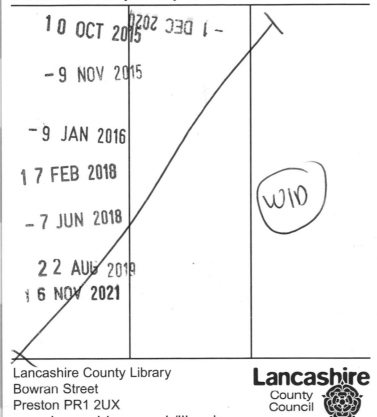

Scholastic Children's Books,
Euston House, 24 Eversholt Street,
London, NW1 1DB, UK

A division of Scholastic Ltd
London ~ New York ~ Toronto ~ Sydney ~ Auckland
Mexico City ~ New Delhi ~ Hong Kong

Published by Scholastic Ltd, 2015

Text © Nick Arnold, 2015
(except text on pages 30–31 © Tony De Saulles)
Illustration © Tony De Saulles, 2015

ISBN 978 1407 15654 5

Printed and bound in Germany

Some of the material in this annual has previously been published in the *Horrible Science* books
© Nick Arnold and Tony De Saulles
Famously Foul Experiments
The Horrible Science of Everything
How to Draw Horrible Science
Chemical Chaos
Space, Stars & Slimy Aliens
The Awfully Big Quiz Book

HORRIBLE SCIENCE

ANNUAL 2016

Nick Arnold and Tony De Saulles

SCHOLASTIC

This Horrible Annual belongs to:

CONTENTS

WHICH MAD SCIENTIST ARE YOU?

Would you prefer to work in a lab or out in the field?

Never! I want everyone to know how clever I am. After all I've worked hard for the glory.

Do other people try to take credit for your work?

Of course! A true scientist should be willing to collect saliva from a rabid dog with his own mouth or expose herself to radiation poisoning.

All the time! People always assume my work was done by someone else (usually a man!).

Are you willing to sacrifice your health/safety/life for your experiments?

Is your family full of scientists or are you the odd one out?

No way! I'll stick to things that can be worked out on paper.

Yes, I am very charming and like to be the centre of attention.

Do you care about being popular and adored?

No, I prefer to focus on my work and am happy in my own company.

Do you always turn up on time for school and do well in all your lessons?

8

I'd like to explore the world by ship for five years gathering samples for my work.

You're Charles Darwin (1809-1882)

You are the British naturalist and geologist famous for your theories of evolution and natural selection. You discovered that people are descended from apes. You travelled round the world by ship to study fossils and skeletons (even though you got very seasick!).

I'd rather work from my own, clean laboratory in Paris. Preferably alone.

You're Louis Pasteur (1822-1895)

You are the famous French chemist and microbiologist who studied germs. You created a vaccine for rabies (by testing it on a 9-yr-old boy!) and persuaded doctors to clean their hands before surgery. You also developed a technique for stopping milk going off – now called Pasteurization after you.

Five members of my family have won Nobel Prizes (I won two!).

You're Marie Curie (1867-1934)

You are the amazing scientist who studied radioactivity. You discovered two new elements (polonium and radium) and were the first woman to win a Nobel Prize. Sadly, you didn't realize how dangerous your experiments were and died of radiation poisoning.

My father was a famous poet, but my mother pushed me to do mathematics so I didn't turn out like him.

You're Ada Lovelace (1815-1852)

You are the world's first computer programmer. You worked with Charles Babbage on his early computer, but you had much more vision than all the men. Your father was the famous poet, Lord Byron. The computer language 'Ada' is named after you. You are very well off, and marry an Earl.

Yes. I excel at everything and have even been described as "alarmingly clever"!

You're Rosalind Franklin (1920-1958)

You are the British chemist who was involved in the discovery of the structure of DNA. You should have won a Nobel Prize, but you died young and the men hogged the limelight.

No. I don't enjoy school and hate how strict it is. I prefer learning in my own way.

You're Albert Einstein (1879-1955)

You are the famous German physicist who came up with the Theory of Relativity. You moved to America to escape the Nazis. You won a Nobel Prize in 1921. You were also very musical, and played the violin and piano. Your name is now used to mean 'genius'.

THE BRAIN-BOGGLING BIG BANG

Everything started with a Big Bang. That's how scientists describe the moment the universe popped out of nothing 13.7 billion years ago. But what was nothing like? Well here's a brain-bending experiment to show you the answer...

A thought experiment is an experiment that scientists imagine in their heads. All you need to try one is...

ONE BRAIN (IDEALLY YOUR OWN).

THINK! IMAGINE! DREAM! CALCULATE!

WARNING! These experiments are guaranteed not to make a mess, but don't think too hard or brain juice might squirt from your ears...

SQURP!

Horrible thought experiment – lots of fuss about nothing...

Imagine you're a magician and you make your pet rabbit Mr Fluffy vanish. That's right! You pop him into a top hat, wave your magic wand and ABRACADABRA, hey presto – the hat is empty! There's nothing in it!

Now imagine a harder trick. This time you stuff the universe into your hat and make that disappear too!

WOW – now there's NOTHING around you! There's no light and no dark, no space and no time. In fact there's nothing at all. Er, hold on – there's no air to breathe, so you'd better bring the universe back pretty quick!

STAGE 1

HEY – YOU'LL GIVE ME A NOSE BLEED!

STAGE 2

GASP!

Nothing sounded a bit scary, didn't it? I bet you wouldn't want to spend the weekend there. But before the universe there really was nothing at all.

SO WHY DID THE UNIVERSE BEGIN?

BEWARE! You should **NEVER** ask a scientist this question! If you do, they might gibber and froth at the mouth or, even worse, they might start mumbling about virtual particles in quantum foam and things that happened in other dimensions… The truth is, no one's too sure why it happened. All I can say is that the Big Bang would have been BIG news – if there'd been any newspapers to report it…

The COSMIC CHRONICLE

WIN A SPACE HOLIDAY!

EXCLUSIVE!

— 13.7 billion years BC —

Also in this week's issue…
The universe – what it means for you!
Space - what's the big deal?

THE UNIVERSE IS BORN!

Time and space started this morning with a Big Bang. Said one eyewitness, "It came from nowhere. One moment it wasn't there – the next moment it was!! It gave me a nasty turn, I can tell you! Things like that shouldn't be allowed especially as it was billions of degrees and I'm a bit cooked now."

The editor writes…
Nothing like the universe has ever happened before – well, nothing's ever happened before. This could be the start of something really BIG!

Mind you, the Big Bang wasn't actually a bang at all. There was no air to carry the sound so it wasn't as loud as your dad snoring. Oh dear, I hope you're not too disappointed…

THE SCARY SOLAR SYSTEM

We're off to see the Solar System – that's the Sun and its surrounding planets. And we'll be seeking out a stack of stunning Solar System secrets to make you starry-eyed...

EARTH (diameter 12,756 km)
Pretty planet. Must get round to visiting it some day.

MARS (diameter 6,780 km)
The only difference between Mars and a freeze-dried pea is that Mars is bigger and you can't eat it. Mars has four times more craters than the Moon, including one called Galle that looks like a smiley face.

SUN
(diameter 1.4 million km)
The Sun is 99.8 per cent of the mass of the Solar System. That means the Earth, you, me, Mr Fluffy and the other planets are just measly, crummy leftovers.

MERCURY
(diameter 4,878 km)
The innermost planet whizzes round the Sun at 172,248 km per hour. And what's more, it NEVER gets dizzy!

VENUS (diameter 12,100 km)
The Sun rises in the west and sets in the east on Venus because it spins in the opposite direction to the other planets. One Venus day lasts 243 Earth days, which means that school days on Venus are a real drag.

GRR — FOOLISH NON-SCIENTISTS CLAIM A HILL ON MARS IS A FACE MADE BY ALIENS, BUT IT'S JUST A TRICK OF THE LIGHT!

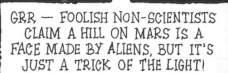

MOON (diameter 3,476 km)
Each year the Moon creeps away from the Earth. It only moves 4 cm but that means in five billion years' time the Moon will be heading for Venus. Mind you, we'll be toast by then.

THE PURPLE SLOBWOBBLER ON A RARE VISIT TO THE SOLAR SYSTEM

SVERK SHMIK BIPPLE ZNIFF*

*ERK! AN UGLY SPACE MONSTER!

CHEEK!

JUPITER (diameter 143,000 km) Big J is so stunningly sizeable that you can fit all the other planets inside it with room to spare. Or, if you preferred, you could squash 1,300 Earths into it. (So where do we find 1,299 more Earths?)

NEPTUNE (diameter 49,000 km) and the dwarf planet **PLUTO** (diameter about 2,400 km) Pluto's orbit actually crosses Neptune's, so these two planets take it in turns to be furthest from the Sun. If you flew a plane to Neptune, it would take over 289 years to get there. The flight to Pluto would take 370 years. Hmm – I hope the in-flight movies are good.

URANUS (diameter 52,000 km) Unlike every other planet, Uranus rolls head over heels rather than spinning. No wonder it's a bit blue…

THE ASTEROID BELT Made up of one billion space rocks that were left over when the Solar System formed. If one hits us, we'll be rocked… The largest is the dwarf planet Ceres – it's over 930 km across.

SATURN (diameter 120,000 km) Soaraway Saturn is mostly hydrogen and helium. I guess you could paint a face on Saturn and turn it into a giant helium balloon.

KUIPER BELT and **ERIS** The Kuiper Belt consists of icy rubble left over from the making of the Solar System. Eris is a distant dwarf planet – it's the ultimate get-away holiday destination.

BET YOU NEVER KNEW!

1. There's a stunning amount of space in the Solar System. If Earth was the size of this marble, Mars would be the size of a freeze-dried pea 50 metres away.

2. The fastest human machines ever, the Voyager space probes, travelled at 56,000 km per hour, but they took nine years to reach Uranus and 12 years to get as far as Pluto's orbit. It's enough to space out your brain!

MARS. The planet's red colour comes from iron oxide in the rocks, ground down over millions of years to form a fine, red soil. Strong winds create dust storms which give the atmosphere its red tinge. Try this experiment to get an idea of what to expect on Mars...

Dare you discover ... how to cause a Martian dust storm?

You will need:

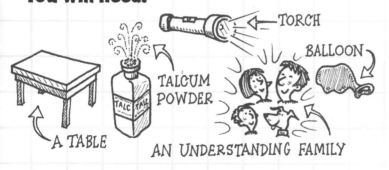

TORCH
BALLOON
TALCUM POWDER
A TABLE
AN UNDERSTANDING FAMILY

What you do:

1 Darken the room or wait until dark. Switch on the torch and place it so that it shines on the table from the side.

2 Sprinkle the table with talcum powder.

3 Blow up the balloon and let out the air a few times.

4 Now blow up the balloon and place the mouth of the balloon so that the escaping air blows over the top of the table.

You should notice:

The dust swirls out in a big cloud, billows into the air and floats about like a 100 per cent genuine Martian dust storm. Great, isn't it? In fact, just like on Mars, the dust storm starts when the wind blows bits of dust against each other that knock into more dust, etc.

Ask permission before blanketing your home in a talcum-powder dust storm. If you don't, you might be sent to Mars, or possibly to your bedroom, until the dust settles!

SATURN. Saturn is famous for its rings, made up of shiny bits of ice and rock. If you don't happen to have a really good telescope, here's the next best way to see them up close:

Dare you discover ... Saturn's rings?

You will need:

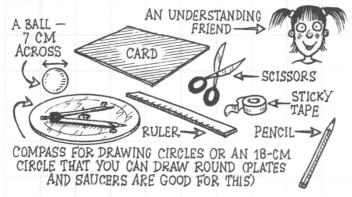

A BALL — 7 CM ACROSS

AN UNDERSTANDING FRIEND →

CARD

← SCISSORS

← STICKY TAPE

RULER →

PENCIL →

COMPASS FOR DRAWING CIRCLES OR AN 18-CM CIRCLE THAT YOU CAN DRAW ROUND (PLATES AND SAUCERS ARE GOOD FOR THIS)

What you do:

1 Using the compass, or an object to draw round, draw a circle on the card 18 cm across. The circle should be 11 cm wider than the ball. Cut the circle out.
2 Cut out the inside of the card circle to make a card ring.

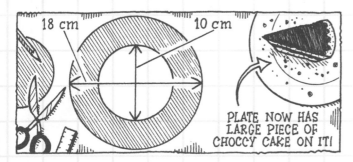

18 cm   10 cm

PLATE NOW HAS LARGE PIECE OF CHOCCY CAKE ON IT!

3 Stick your card ring to the ball with sticky tape.

4 Well done, you've just made Saturn! Ask your friend to hold it in their hand and stand 15 metres away from you. They should start by holding the planet level and then at an angle.

USE CHOCOLATE CAKE AS A BRIBE

YUM!

LIKE THIS

CHOMP!   MUNCH!

AND THEN LIKE THIS

You should notice:

When the rings are held level you can't see them. They're too thin and far away. The real Saturn's the same. Saturn spins at an angle, and every 15 years the rings cannot be seen from Earth. In fact, we're looking at Saturn sideways on. But they appear when seen from any other angle...

BET YOU NEVER KNEW!

Saturn's rings are 270,000 km wide, but only 30 metres thick. If you put the rings in a giant shrinking machine and shrank them to the size of a cricket or baseball pitch, they'd be no thicker than this page.

HOW TO BE A STAR ASTRONAUT IN FIVE EASY LESSONS

So you want to explore the breathtakingly BIG universe? Great – you've come to the right place! Why not join our scientists on our astronaut training course?

THE HORRIBLE SCIENCE ASTRONAUT TRAINING COURSE

Lesson 1 – Driving a rocket ain't rocket science

All you do is switch on the engine...

Hot gases blast out this end

X-ray view

BOOSH!

BLAM!

Hot gases blast against inner walls of rocket

Rocket is pushed forward

EEK! WHERE'S THE STEERING WHEEL?

Your rocket doesn't have brakes or a steering wheel. To change your course, you fire another rocket engine in the opposite direction to the one you want to travel.

Lesson 2 – Being weightless

Away from Earth's gravity, your body is weightless. And that means everything in your body, including your half-digested sick and blood, will be weightless too. You may notice some unusual changes as your body fluids float upwards...

Legs and waist shrink

Nose feels blocked

Puffy eyes

Fluids float to kidneys, causing an urge to wee

Lesson 3 – Take a breather

There's no air in space. This can be a problem, since your spacecraft can get very smelly - especially if a fellow astronaut has been scoffing beans. If your head hurts, and you gasp and feel sick, this could be due to the smell - or it could be due to a dangerous build-up of carbon-dioxide gas breathed out by your body. Use lithium salt to soak up the carbon dioxide - but remember, there's one thing you should NEVER do...

I'LL JUST OPEN THE WINDOW!

Lesson 4 – Living with weightlessness

Being weightless has good and bad sides...

• **GOOD SIDE** You can perform superb somersaults and awesome acrobatics, and play weird games like upside-down, slow motion darts.

• **BAD SIDE** Your brain gets confused about which way up you should be. This causes dizziness, sweating and throwing up.

• It's so easy to float around that your muscles and bones don't have much work to do. They start to waste away and you need to exercise for two hours a day to keep them strong.

• Anything you spill forms round globules and floats around your spacecraft. An accident on the space toilet doesn't bear thinking about.

IT'S FUN CATCHING THESE CHOCOLATE PEANUTS!

Lesson 5 – Coming back is hard to do

Sooner or later you'll want to go home – after all, there's only so much floating around in a metal box that you can take. But the return to Earth is actually the most dangerous part of your mission... When your spacecraft hits the atmosphere, it's moving so fast that air molecules can't get out of the way. They're shoved together in front of the craft and heat up by rubbing (friction). Your craft heats up too, and it could burn up. Hopefully your craft's heat shields will protect you – but if not, your goose is cooked, and that goes for the rest of you! Still wanna be an astronaut?

BET YOU NEVER KNEW!
In 1963 astronaut Gordon Cooper circled the Earth 22 times in his spacecraft. Part of his mission was to take a sample of his wee for testing. Unfortunately, the wee escaped and floated around inside his smelly spacecraft.

NO WAY!

COMET GET IT!

Are you up to the toughest challenge in the Solar System? Your mission is pilot the high-tech radio-controlled Rosetta probe around the Solar System and land a mini-probe on a COMET millions of kilometres away. In 2014 scientists at the European Space Agency managed to do it. Could you beat the same challenges?

Solar panels to make electricity from sunlight

Philae - lander

Thrusters to control flight

Radio equipment to send and collect signals from Earth

February 2004
1 Your first job is to get Rosetta into space – how do you do it?
a) Fly it like a plane.
b) Stick it on a rocket.

December 2005
2 As Rosetta flies away from the Sun, its batteries get less solar power. How can you stop them running down?
a) Switch on a built-in sunray lamp.
b) Put Rosetta on stand-by mode (just like a TV).

December 2006
3 Rosetta has developed a couple of mechanical faults. What do you do?
a) Carry on with a few remote-controlled adjustments.
b) Ask astronauts from the International Space Station to do the work.

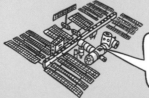

MAYBE LATER – WE'RE EATING OUR DINNER!

November 2007
4 Rosetta is heading for Mars. Your priceless probe could crash! How do you react?
a) Cross your fingers and order the probe to take a close look at the red planet.
b) Take a detour to avoid the perilous planet.

August 2008 and July 2010
5 You order Rosetta to take a close look at asteroids (giant space rocks). What are you looking for?
a) Aliens
b) Minerals

18

November 2009

6 Rosetta is whizzing around Earth. Why bring the space probe close to home when it's supposed to be chasing a comet?

a) You wanted to check that the probe is all right.

b) You wanted to boost its speed by whirling it round Earth like a slingshot.

August 2014

7 This is it – after an epic trek, Rosetta is close to the comet. THE COMET IS CRAZY. It looks like a giant rubber duck doing somersaults! The comet is so far off it takes twenty minutes for your radio signal orders to get through and it's speeding at 18 km per SECOND. How on Earth can you land Philae? Sorry I meant "how on comet can you land Philae?"

a) Easy, I wait for it to stop somersaulting.

b) I just hope I get my timing right.

October 2014

8 The comet is covered in cliffs and boulders and there are weird gas jets coming off it. If you pick the wrong landing site Philae will be smashed – what's the plan?

a) Ask the public to pick a landing site – that way if Philae crashes you don't get the blame.

b) Calmly select a site on the "head" of the comet. It looks smoother.

HERE!

November 2014

Philae sets off to land on the comet. It's taken ten years, five months and four days to get here. Rosetta has been round the Sun five times and travelled 6.4 billion km. The whole world watches and holds its breath. The billion euro mission is at stake. You anxiously wait for news ... and wait ... and at last you get a MESSAGE FROM PHILAE. YOU'VE DONE IT – YES! YOU'VE LANDED ON A COMET!!!!!!

9 Er, now what?

a) It's job done – let's PARTY!

b) You want to watch interesting science experiments.

WOOHOO!

December 2014

Philae didn't just land – it bounced twice and ended up in the shadow of a cliff. Cut off from sunlight power – the lander went into standby mode. At least it did some experiments. Meanwhile Rosetta tested water ice coming off the comet and found that it has a different chemistry to the water on Earth.

10 What's your plan for the next year?

a) Get a job selling comet mineral water at 10 million euros a bottle.

b) Wait for the comet to get closer to the Sun. Perhaps Philae will wake up if there's more sunlight.

Well, whatever you decide one thing's for sure. The Rosetta mission isn't over. It is set to continue throughout 2015!

STAR-STRUCK STAR-SPOTTER'S COMPETITION

Here's your chance to prove you know one end of a telescope from the other!

How to play

1 Study the Space-spotter's guide below.

2 Spot the objects listed and note down their co-ordinates in the star grid – for example, there's a red giant star in square A1.

WARNING: THERE MAY BE MORE THAN ONE OF EACH OBJECT!

3 Check your answers on page 56 and GOOD LUCK!

SPACE-SPOTTER'S GUIDE

1 Red giants
No, we're not in the land of fairy tales. A red giant is what happens when a star like the Sun runs out of hydrogen.

2 White dwarf
What's left after a red giant's blown itself out. That's how our poor old Sun's going to end up.

3 Red dwarf
A dim star one-tenth the size of the Sun.

4 Brown dwarf
A wannabe star that never got big enough to shine. It probably sits around all day feeling sorry for itself.

5 Supernova
A giant exploding star that goes pop with the force of 1,000 billion atom bombs. If one went off closer than 33 light years away we'd get roasted by X-rays and gamma rays. DON'T PANIC READERS! We're not that close to one of these nasty blasters!

6 Neutron star
After the blast what's left of the giant star shrinks to the size of a large city under its own gravity. The gigantic gravity of a neutron star means a tiny microbe would weigh as much as two ocean liners.

7 Black hole
A star with ten times more mass than the Sun doesn't end up as a neutron star. Its giant gravity sucks a hole in the universe. This horrible hole is black because not even speedy light can escape. So everything gets sucked in – planets, stars, moons, asteroids and the astronauts' baked beans.

8 Quasar (Kway-zar)
Galaxies form around huge black holes that slurp in stars like giant plugholes. As matter whirls into the black hole it heats up and vast explosions result. This is a quasar, but your legs needn't turn to jelly – the nearest quasars are billions of light years away.

20

9 Galaxy
Some galaxies are shaped like spirals and some look like alien flying saucers. How many of each can you spot?

10 The Milky Way
Our friendly local galaxy is spiral-shaped, but the area where there's the most stars looks like a giant's dribble to us because we see it from the side. We're about 25,000 light years from the black hole that probably lurks in the centre.

11 Andromeda galaxy
This spiral galaxy is two billion light years off, but it's heading our way. In the time it's taken you to read about it, it's whizzed 1,000 km closer. DON'T SCREAM! It won't hit us for five billion years and when it does, most of the stars will pass each other (space is big enough to avoid collisions).

12 Alien planets
Planets may be common in the Milky Way but there's no proof that aliens live on them.

According to one guess, planets with intelligent life on them could be 200 light years apart, so the aliens probably won't be dropping in for coffee... By the way, can you spot the purple slobwobbler alien in the vastness of space?

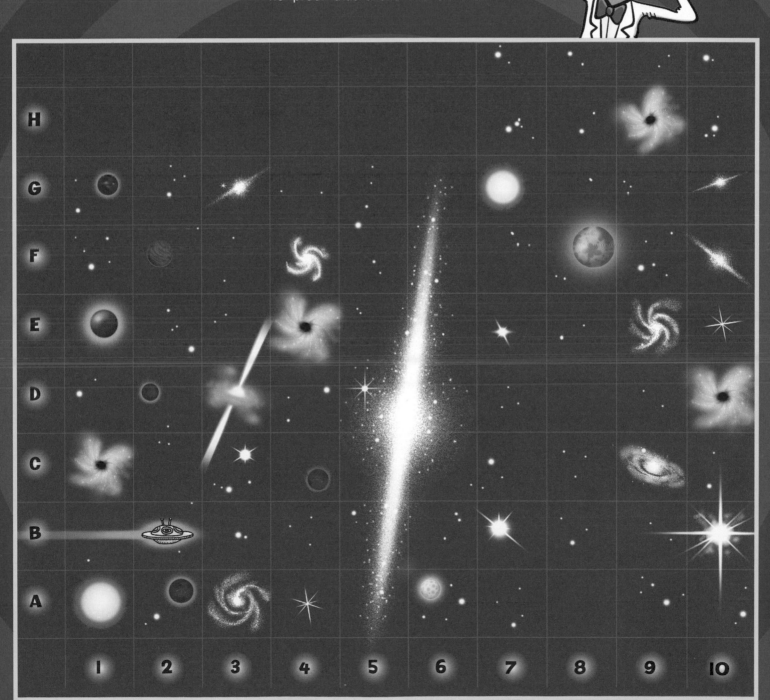

TOP TEN DREADFUL DINOSAUR DISCOVERIES

Back in the days when your teacher was young, they didn't have to remember too many tongue-twisting dino names. But now scientists know of over one thousand dinos and hardly a month goes by without some new dino coming to light. Here's a countdown of our favourite new dino discoveries!

TEN

It's official – dinos were colourful characters. Scientists have looked at the remains of dinosaur fossil feathers through microscopes and compared them to present-day bird feathers. It turns out some dinos were black and others brown-red. One even had orange and white stripes. Show-off!

NINE

Ever wondered where dinosaurs lived? I mean dinos didn't live in houses because they hadn't been invented. Scientists have found out some dinos lived in burrows. Oryctodromeus (or-ric-to-dro-me-us) dug holes in the forest … partly using its nose as a shovel! Sounds like a "hole" lot of pain.

EIGHT

Imagine a T. Rex. Scary huh? Now imagine it covered in feathers. Not so scary now? Hmm – I don't know. Yutyranus (you-ty-ran-us) is a newly discovered Asian T. Rex relative that was covered in feathers. It looked like a giant bad-attitude budgie. Just don't say "who's a pretty dino?" and offer it budgie seed!

SEVEN

Actually T. Rex had lots of rotten relatives and they're popping up all over the world. We like one found in Utah, USA, called Lythronax (li-throw-nax). The name means "King of Gore". If you got too close to this eight-metre 2.5 tonne murder munching machine you might end up saying "Gore Blimey"!

Hi, Uncle T!

SIX

In dino times school swimming lessons must have been even more terrifying than today. Spinosaurus (spi-no-sor-rus) (the dino with a sail on its back) was a bit of a dino swimming champ. This toothy terror had a head like a crocodile and its body was longer than a T. Rex. It probably scrunched sharks for snacks.

FIVE

In 2014 scientists found the skeleton of Dreadnoughtus (dred-nort-us) – the biggest dino yet found. This 26 metre-long super-sized salad-scoffer was a suaropod (long necked and long tailed) dino weighing seven times more than a T. Rex. Your school veg patch wouldn't last one minute. Just imagine one in a zoo – would you want to shovel up its massive poo mountains?

FOUR

Rhinorex – yes, really – was a plant-eating dino with a giant snout. The name means "nose king". Can you imagine King Nosey getting a cold? Scientists reckon the male may have used its stupendous schnozzle to impress female dinos. I bet they were blown away – especially when it sneezed!

THREE

OK – can anyone tell me what's with the hat? This is Kosmoceratops (kos-mor-ser-ra-tops), a show-off relative of Triceratops from Utah. Scientists think males used the ridiculous headgear to impress females. Or it might just be some kind of dino fashion disaster.

TWO

So what is it? If you say "the smelly backside of a pantomime horse that got eaten by crocodile" we'll give you half a mark for humour. Everything about this dinosaur is weird. Its arms were found fifty years before the rest of it. And it's got a weird name, Deinocheirus mirificus (Die-no-ki-rus mir-rif-fic-us) – meaning "unusual horrible hand". If it came from a junk shop – it would be "horrible second-hand hand".

ONE

Everyone knows that dinos couldn't fly – right? Wrong! In 2012 scientists found a dinosaur called Microraptor (my-cro-rap-tor) with FOUR wings! Scientists thought the winged wonder used its wings to turn whilst legging it. Then they built a model Microraptor and proved the dino could glide down from trees.

SPOT THE DIFFERENCE

ERK!

GRARGH!

GRARGH!

GRRRR!

SPLOOSH!

BLFURGH!

DON'T WORRY, IT'S ONLY A TIDDLER!

SCRUNCH!

Can you find 10 differences between these two pictures of scary prehistoric sealife?

D-DAY FOR DINOSAURS

Sixty-five million years ago dinosaurs became extinct. Scientists think Earth was whacked by an asteroid several kilometres across.

An **asteroid** is a lump of space rock.

Extinction is when a species dies out.

Here's how a young Pachycephalosaurus might have remembered the disaster...

65 million years ago
North America

Dear Mum,
What a terrible day! Me and the herd were snacking on leaves when a light streaked across the sky brighter than the Sun! One second later came a super-hot blast with the force of seven billion atom bombs. The sky went black and we were blown off our feet. No sooner had I got up when I was bashed on the head by burning rocks. (It sometimes helps to be a thickhead!) Anyway that was this morning but even now it's raining acid, and umbrellas haven't been invented yet! The weather forecast is cold for 10,000 years, plus lots of choking gas from volcanoes... Now call me a thick-headed lizard, but something tells me things aren't looking too good for us dinosaurs. Is this the end of the AAAARRRRGGGGH!

But the end of the dinosaurs was good news for US. During the dinosaur era, your ancestors were tiny, timid and terrified. But after the asteroid did for the dinosaurs, the mammals bounded from their burrows and took over the Earth. Yes, if it wasn't for that lovely lump of space rock, you could be 5 cm long and live in a hole...

After the dinosaurs a whole host of curious creatures evolved...

1 Titanis was a 2.5-metre-tall fearsome flesh-eating bird that lived 50 million years ago. It sounds nasty enough to give your pet cat personality problems and I bet it had a fowl temper.

2 Imagine a guinea pig as big as a bad-tempered buffalo. In 2002 scientists found the remains of this creature in Venezuela. Just be grateful you don't have to clean out its cage.

3 The Paraceratherium (pa-ra-sera-thee-ree-um) of 35 million years ago was a sort of rhino the size of a house. At 8 metres tall it was the largest land mammal ever.

4 The Australian Procoptodon (pro-kop-toe-don) was a 3-metre-tall killer kangeroo. If it caught you on the hop, you'd be in for the high jump.

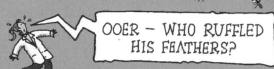

OOER — WHO RUFFLED HIS FEATHERS?

And so, at last...

Seven million years ago, in Africa, an obscure primate stood on its hind legs and learnt how to make tools. Slowly it became smarter. It evolved into new species that learnt how to use fire and wear clothes and grow crops and read *Horrible Science* books and become YOU. Now that's what I call progress! In 2001 African scientist Ahounta Djimdoumalbaye discovered the remains of a prehistoric primate that lived in east Africa over six million years ago. This could have been one of our most ancient ancestors.

DINO MAYHEM
Can you find 10 bug scientists hiding in the chaos?

THE ART OF HORRIBLE SCIENCE

Want to learn how to draw deadly dinosaurs? You've come to the right place! You will need: a soft pencil (2B pencils are good), a black felt-tip pen, a soft rubber and coloured pens or pencils. Draw a pencil outline first and then add the detail. When you're happy with your drawing, go over it in ink. When the ink is dry, rub out the pencil.

CHOMP!

Powerful back legs

Razor-sharp teeth

Small front legs

Small head on big body

Typical meat-eating dinosaur

Typical meat-eater eating a typical plant-eater

CHOMP!

Typical plant-eating dinosaur

Flat teeth for grinding plants

Huge, oval-shaped body

Long neck for reaching plants in treetops

Big tail to balance weight of long neck

Legs like an elephant

And for dino-boffins who want to draw dinosaurs with real names...

T Rex

Ankylosaurus

Triceratops

Stegosaurus

Two more prehistoric creatures...

Pterosaur   **Plesiosaur**

Wings
with
claws

Beak
with
teeth

Huge flippers
for swimming

EEK, I'M FLYING AND
IT'S PTERO—FYING!

HAVE YOU
MET MY
COUSIN IN
LOCH NESS?

EVOLUTION MADE EASY

Evolution explains how animals change over thousands of years. In a moment we'll meet the brilliant barnacle-brained boffin who figured it out – but first let's find out where DNA comes from. Take a look at your family tree...

Where your DNA came from...

SQURP!
3.85 billion years ago — slimy microbe

FLOBBLE!
2.5 billion years ago — something that looked like a jellyfish

SWIGGLE!
520 million years ago — eel-like creature

GRARR!
400 million years ago — ugly-looking fish

GRURK!
300 million years ago — giant amphibian

240 million years ago — hairy reptile

SQWEEK!
50 million years ago — ancient primate, a furry creature that lived in trees

SSSS!
100 million years ago — small rat-like mammal

EEP!

7 million years ago — ape-like creature

HOO HOO!

UG!
2 million years ago — early humans

STUNNED SILENCE!
100,000 years ago — modern humans = YOU!

And here are the full fascinating facts about how all these creatures evolved over time and ended up as you...

HORRIBLE SCIENCE FACT FILE

Name: How evolution works

THE BASIC FACTS:
• DNA is the code that controls your appearance.
• Every animal has its own special DNA code that it passes on to its young.
• The DNA code can be changed (for example, by damaging chemicals). Other changes can happen when DNA is copied to make new cells. Changes to the code make the offspring look different.
• For an animal, every day is a battle to find food and avoid being food for another beast (if you don't believe me, just ask Mr Fluffy). Animals with features that help them in this battle are more likely to breed and pass on these advantages in their DNA.
• Over time all the animals in this species will take on the new, improved features…

THE HORRIBLE DETAILS:
If just one of all these creatures that were your ancestors hadn't mated and passed on their DNA, you wouldn't exist today!

NEW IMPROVED EARS!

Hmm, what an incredible idea! I bet you'd just love to meet the gobsmacking genius who thought it up?

Brainy Boffin

Charles Darwin (1809–1882)

Charles's dad told his son, "You'll be a disgrace to yourself and all your family." He didn't like his son's hobbies of shooting and rat catching, but actually young Darwin was into science too. At school he was nicknamed "Gas" because he liked chemistry, and he later became interested in nature.
Darwin's ideas about evolution took shape after a five-year voyage round the world when he was young man, but he didn't get round to making them public until 1858. The work might have been easier for Darwin if he'd known about genes, but they weren't widely known until the 1900s.

BET YOU NEVER KNEW!
Before he wrote his book on evolution, Darwin spent eight years studying barnacles. He kept 10,000 of them in tanks at home. I bet they got in the way and his wife told him off...

ELEMENTARY ELEMENTS

Different varieties of atoms are known as elements. For years chemical knowledge was in chaos as confused chemists tried to classify these chemicals.

Chaotic chemical elements

You can find 92 elements on Earth. More elements are made in nuclear reactors or created by scientists out of tiny bits of matter. But the heavier man-made elements have the rather irritating habit of falling apart after a second. Here's your very own chaotic guide to elements that don't do this.

CHAOTIC ELEMENTS SPOTTER'S GUIDE

Name of element:
ALUMINIUM

Where found: in soil and rocks

Crucial characteristics: a light and useful metal. It's used to make tank armour, saucepans, kitchen foil and folding chairs. You can even make clothes out of it! HATS TOO

Name of element:
CALCIUM

Where found: milk, chalk and marble and also in bones and the plaster used to set broken bones.

Crucial characteristics: if you burn calcium it gives off a lovely red flame. But that's no excuse for setting fire to your teacher's plastered toe! OOH LOVELY!

Name of element:
CARBON

Where found: in diamonds, benzene, coal and the "lead" in your pencil.

Crucial characteristics: the most common atom in the human body, which is a bit weird, because people don't look anything like lumps of coal. I DO

Name of element:
LEAD

Where found: This isn't the lead in your pencil. Real lead is a grey metal often found on old church roofs.

Crucial characteristics: it's quite a nasty poison if you happened to eat it by mistake. It's also very heavy so don't go dropping it on your teacher's toe.

Name of element:
COPPER

Where found: in rocks under the ground.

Crucial characteristics: lots of uses including electrical wires and the rivets that hold your jeans together. Air pollution caused by cars and industry causes a chemical reaction that turns copper green. That's why the copper plated Statue of Liberty in New York looks a bit sea-sick. GET ME A BUCKET

Name of element:
CHLORINE

Where found: in salt, sea water and rock salt.

Crucial characteristics: it's very good for killing germs, but not very nice if it gets up your nose.

Name of element: GOLD

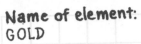

Where found: in rocks under the ground.

Crucial characteristics: gold is good to make into jewellery – that's why people drape it round their necks. It's also worth lots of dosh.

Name of element: SILVER

Where found: in underground rocks.

Crucial characteristics: a really useful shiny metal much prized for dangling around the neck, making the shiny backs of mirrors and really posh cutlery. In the last 50 years people have lost 100,000 tonnes of silver coins. Where have they all got to? That's what I'd like to know.

> I'VE NO IDEA – HONEST!

Name of element: PLUTONIUM

Where found: it's found in nuclear reactors but nowhere else in nature.

Crucial characteristics: Plutonium is incredibly poisonous. It looks like metal but it turns green in the air. And damp air makes it catch fire! The man who discovered plutonium in 1940 kept a lump of it in a matchbox. Weird.

Name of element: HYDROGEN

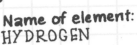

Where found: it's the most common element. Stars such as the Sun are made of hydrogen. So is 97 per cent of the known universe.

Crucial characteristics: hydrogen is also the lightest element so it floats upwards. This was why hydrogen gas was once used in balloons. It's also burnt as a rocket fuel. Hydrogen sulphide is a gas that stinks of rotten eggs. But don't confuse it with a stink bomb – it's poisonous.

Name of element: HELIUM

Where found: in the air

Crucial characteristics: used to fill balloons. It's lighter than air so the balloons float skywards. Breathing helium makes your voice sound like Mickey Mouse. This happens because your voice passes faster through helium than ordinary air. So it sounds higher and squeakier!

Name of element: IRON

Where found: much of the earth is made of iron. You find it in rocks and the soil.

Crucial characteristics: you can use iron to make railings. It's also found in the chemical that gives blood its tasteful red colour.

Name of element: OXYGEN

Where found: it's the most common element on Planet Earth.

Crucial characteristics: it's really lucky that over one fifth of the atoms in the air are oxygen. Without them we'd be more than a little bit dead. Some people think that if they breathe pure oxygen they'll live longer. They must be confused because scientists believe that breathing too much oxygen is bad for you. They say it damages the body, especially the nerves and lungs.

Name of element: SULPHUR

Where found: sulphur is a smelly yellow chemical spat out of volcanoes in choking clouds.

Crucial characteristics: at one time it was known as brimstone and mixed with treacle. It was used as a medicine for children. The medicine tasted disgusting so it was probably spat out by the choking children too.

Odd elements quiz

Some of the more obscure elements are ever so odd. Which of these are too strange to be true?

True or false

1 The element phosphorous was discovered by an alchemist whilst he was examining the contents of his own urine.

2 The elements yttrium, erbium, terbium and ytterbium are all named after a quarry in Sweden.

3 The element dysprosium was discovered in 1886. The Greek name means "really smelly".

4 The element selenium was discovered by the Swedish scientist Berzelius. Sadly, he didn't realize it was poisonous until it poisoned him!

5 The element cadmium was discovered when it accidentally got into a bottle of medicine.

6 The element krypton was named after the planet that Superman comes from.

7 The scientist who discovered beryllium named it after his wife – Beryl.

8 The element Astatine is so rare that if you searched the entire world you'd only find 0.16 grams of it.

9 Technetium was first found in caterpillar droppings.

10 Lutetium is named after the ancient Roman name for Paris.

See page 57 for the answers.

ON THE CARDS

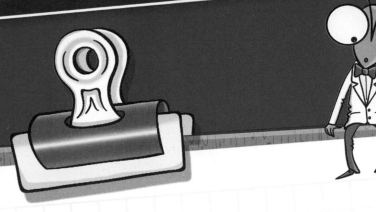

BRAINY BREAKTHROUGH

Name: Dmitri Mendeleyev (1834–1907)

Nationality: Russian

Dmitri Mendeleyev was a big fan of the card game Patience, and that's where he got the idea of writing the names of elements on cards and putting them in weight order. Dmitri created a crucial chart called the Periodic Table, and the number patterns in this tremendous table are a code that explains why certain chemicals combine to create chemical changes. Here's your chance to crack the code...

Here's a card game based on how Dmitri Mendeleyev sorted the elements...

You will need:

- This book • Scissors
- Photocopier
- A good friend (but in an emergency your long-suffering pet adult will do)
- Notebook and pencil

What you do:

1 Photocopy the next page – ideally on to thin card.

2 Cut out the squares. Each one is a card for the game.

3 Read the rules and play the game.

4 After the game lay down all the cards to complete the columns. Arrange the columns so that the rows are in order of number – so Li will be next to Be and Na next to Mg and so on.

1

H

HYDROGEN

2

He

HELIUM

3

Li

LITHIUM

4

Be

BERYLLIUM

5

B

BORON

6

C

CARBON

7

N

NITROGEN

8

O

OXYGEN

9

F

FLUORINE

10

Ne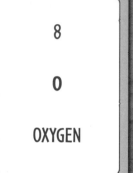

NEON

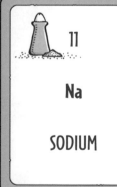

11

Na

SODIUM

12

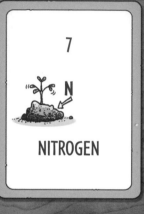 **Mg**

MAGNESIUM

13

Al

ALUMINIUM

14

Si

SILICON

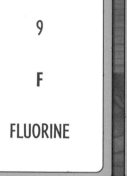

15

P

PHOSPHORUS

16

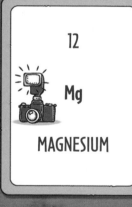 **S**

SULPHUR

17

Cl

CHLORINE

18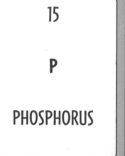

Ar

ARGON

Atomic Eights

Rules of the game

1 Shuffle the cards. Give yourself and your friend 9 cards each.

2 The player with the H = hydrogen starts off by laying this card face up. They are followed by the player with the He = Helium card. The player with the Li = Lithium card places it under the Hydrogen card (of course the same player might have all of these cards!)

3 The players each then play a card in turn – the aim is to form as many columns of 2 or 3 as you can. HINT – You can tell which cards go in which column because the lower card is 8 more than the upper. So if you had Be = Beryllium which is 4 you would need Mg = Magnesium to make a column.

4 A player scores TWO points for completing a column of two and THREE points for completing a column of three. But if they put a card in the wrong place they LOSE one point! Write down your scores in the notebook.

5 The game ends when one of the players runs out of cards.

WHAT HAPPENS:

You've actually made a copy of part of the Periodic Table!

THIS IS BECAUSE:

The number of an element (scientists call this the atomic number) is in order of weight – hydrogen is the lightest, so it's number 1. The elements in each column combine with other elements in a similar way. "But why?" I hear you wondering. "And is it to do with the number 8?" Well, yes it is. Imagine two atoms combining to form a molecule Well, to do it, the elements in your game need to share a total of – wait for it – EIGHT electrons! Mind you, Mendeleyev didn't know about all this – electrons hadn't been discovered in his day!

EVIL ELEMENTS

Every element is different, but since this is a *Horrible Science* book we'll be checking out the evil elements that you *definitely* wouldn't want to discover in your dinner... And where better to find evil elements than the nasty notebook of a genuine crazy chemist.

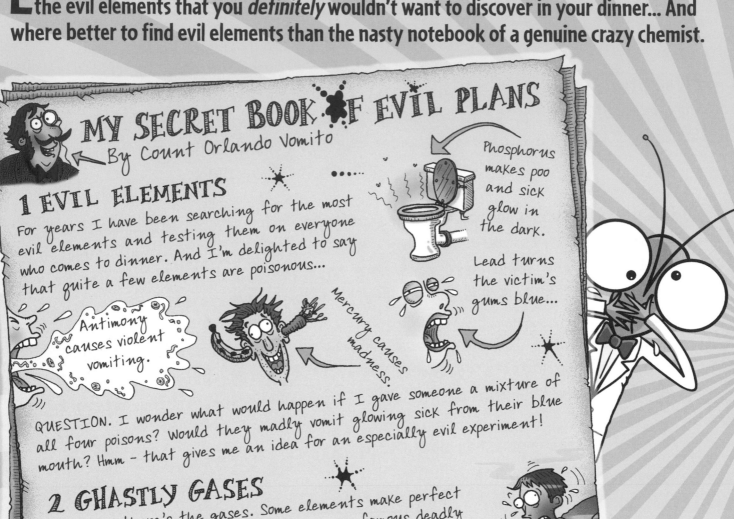

MY SECRET BOOK OF EVIL PLANS
By Count Orlando Vomito

1 EVIL ELEMENTS

For years I have been searching for the most evil elements and testing them on everyone who comes to dinner. And I'm delighted to say that quite a few elements are poisonous...

Phosphorus makes poo and sick glow in the dark.

Lead turns the victim's gums blue...

Antimony causes violent vomiting.

Mercury causes madness.

QUESTION. I wonder what would happen if I gave someone a mixture of all four poisons? Would they madly vomit glowing sick from their blue mouth? Hmm - that gives me an idea for an especially evil experiment!

2 GHASTLY GASES

And then there's the gases. Some elements make perfect poison gases - just right for spicing up my famous deadly dinner parties! For example, there's smelly green chlorine gas. The gas dissolves the lining of the lungs so the victim can't breathe - it's quite a breathtaking sight!

URRRGH!

3 ROTTEN RADIOACTIVITY

If I was feeling really evil, I could try making radioactive poisons. All I'd have to do is zap a nucleus of a radioactive element like uranium with neutrons. The zapped bits of uranium nucleus zap nearby uranium atoms, and the whole thing goes out of control and causes an atomic blast with lots of deadly X-rays and gamma rays! Now that would make my next party go with a bang!

YOU'RE INVITED TO MY RADIOACTIVITY PARTY
IT'LL COST ME A BOMB BUT YOU'LL HAVE A BLAST!

SPOT THE LOT

Can you spot 10 differences between these two pictures of a rotten school science experiment?

IT'S A GAS!

Without gases there'd be chaos. We'd have nothing to breathe and balloons would fall out of the sky. Gases can be chaotic – especially when they poison people or explode! But they're interesting, too. Sometimes they're even funny – take nitrous oxide, for example, better known to you as laughing gas.

... MY CAT WAS RUN OVER ... THE CAR WAS STOLEN ... AND OUR HOUSE BURNT DOWN!

CHEMICAL CHAOS FACT FILE

Name: Gases

The basic facts: Gases are atoms or clumps of atoms that whizz about like tiny balls. You can feel the gas atoms in the air every time you go out in a wind.

Horrible details: Some gases are poisonous.

DARE YOU DISCOVER ... GAS EXPERIMENTS?

1. Want to grab a bit of gas?

You will need:

• A balloon

What you do:

1 Blow up the balloon and pinch the end with your fingers.

2 Squeeze the balloon.

What happens?

a) As you squash more the balloon gets harder to squeeze.

b) As you squash more the balloon gets softer.

c) The balloon stays the same.

2. Make your own gas

You will need:

- A narrow-necked bottle half-filled with water
- A balloon (use the same one!)
- 2 alka-seltzer tablets crushed into powder
- A funnel

What you do:

1 Blow the balloon up and release the air a few times to make it softer.

2 Use the funnel to pour the powdered tablets into the bottle.

3 Quickly stretch the balloon over the neck of the bottle.

4 Very gently swirl the water around in the bottle.

What happens?

a) The balloon is sucked into the bottle.

b) There is a small explosion.

c) The balloon inflates slightly.

3. Bubble trouble

You will need:

- A bottle of fizzy mineral water, lemonade or cola.

What you do:

Give the bottle a really good shake for two minutes.

Slowly open the top and notice what happens.

a) Nothing

b) Loads of bubbles form and gas escapes.

c) Bubbles appear then sink to the bottom.

Answers

1 a) Billions of gas atoms are squashed together. The harder you squeeze, the harder those atoms push back!

2 c) The tablets react with water to make carbon-dioxide gas. The molecules of this gas are made from one carbon and two oxygen atoms joined together.

3 b) The fizz comes from carbon-dioxide bubbles. The gas is dissolved in water under pressure. Removing the top reduces pressure and allows bubbles to form.

BET YOU NEVER KNEW!

Just as in experiment 3, gas bubbles form in the blood of deep sea divers as they surface. The "bends" as they are called can have fatal results! To prevent this, divers spend time in a pressurized chamber so their bodies get used to the change in pressure.

DISGUSTING DISCOVERIES

Every week the world's scientists make more brainy breakthroughs. Here are your favourite *Horrible Science* characters with some brainy and disgusting discoveries ...

SPACE SCIENCE

BRAINY BREAKTHROUGH

What's the biggest thing in the universe? No - it's NOT a big-headed person's head! In 2013 scientists worked out the biggest thing in the universe was THE HERCULES-CORONA BOREALIS GREAT WALL. It's ten billion light years long and made up of thousands of galaxies in a long starry strand.

BUT IT'S TINY!

IDIOT!

DISGUSTING DISCOVERY

In 2012 a space capsule returned to Earth with something strange. What was it? An alien monster? No - it was blood and pee from astronauts. Scientists test them for any body changes due to living in space. I wonder if the astronauts sent back their smelly pants too?

IS IT WEE?

YES - THAT'S WHY I'M USING A MICROSCOPE!

PHYSICS

BRAINY BREAKTHROUGH

In 2012 scientists found the Higg's Boson. Named after British scientist Peter Higgs, who predicted it, this particle is incredibly important. The Higg's Boson affects the space around it to give other particles mass. So it explains why things are made up of matter. In 2013 Peter Higgs was awarded the Nobel Prize.

DISGUSTING DISCOVERY

By 2013 US military scientists developed a new way to control crowds. Known as 'the pain ray', it's a microwave beam that zaps people. A five second zap causes extreme pain. Would you want to test it? Hundreds of people did!

CHEMISTRY

BRAINY BREAKTHROUGH

In 2014 chemists discovered how to break up a molecule of carbon-dioxide (the gas you breathe out) and turn it into oxygen gas that you can breathe (plus one carbon atom). It doesn't sound much - but imagine that you're in space and running out of oxygen. This discovery could be a lifesaver for space travellers!

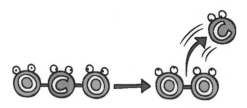

What's big and yellow and lives in sewers? A giant canary with no sense of smell? NO it's worse! It's a giant glob of stinky fat stuck with wet wipes. People pour fat down the toilet and it cools and sets solid. In 2014 a monster glob was found in London. It was as long as a jumbo jet.

THEY MADE ME EAT IT!

FASCINATING!

BIOLOGY

BRAINY BREAKTHROUGH

In 2013 scientists found that you can freeze a blood-sucking leech

I'VE GOT A THAW TONGUE!

at -190°C and even store the frozen freak at -90°C for six months. It comes to life when you thaw it. So would you try this experiment? You could invent the world's first vampire lolly!

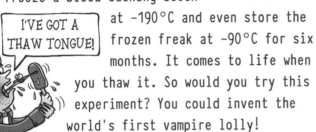

DISGUSTING DISCOVERY

In 2012 scientists in York tested a new food - mashed-up maggot cake. Are you gagging? You will be - the maggots were fed on poo. (Don't worry the revolting recipe is for farm animals and it probably WON'T turn up in your school dinner.)

ROTTEN GRUB!

MEDICINE

BRAINY BREAKTHROUGH

Ever wanted to see your own bones and guts? Scientists at the University of Paris-South, France developed a device that moves your body scan images in time with your movements. You can look in a mirror and admire your insides in gory glory. Fancy a peek?

DISGUSTING DISCOVERY

In 2013 Harvard University scientists studied how changing the food you eat affects bacteria in your guts. They tested microbes in the poo of volunteers. This work was nothing to sniff at (you'd probably need a clothes peg on your nose).

QUICK QUEASY QUIZ

Could you make the next brainy breakthrough? These are REAL science experiments reported in 2014. Just answer the questions - if you can! You'll find the answers on page 58.

1 Why did Norwegian scientists dress up as polar bears?
a) They wanted to scare their mums.
b) They wanted to give reindeer a fright.

2 Scientists at Harvard Medical School, USA taught maths to monkeys (I didn't make this up!) What did they find?
a) The monkeys were smarter than kids.
b) The monkeys could just about add up.

3 What happened when New York scientists zapped a certain area of a man's brain with electricity?
a) He developed X-ray vision.
b) He thought he was in a pizza restaurant.

DODGY DISCOVERIES

A chaotic combination of muddles, mishaps and mix-ups – that's how many a vital substance has been discovered. Scientists have to keep their minds open to anything that might happen during an experiment, but sometimes they might set out to answer one question and end up solving another.

CHAOTIC CHEMISTS' COMMENTS...

Here's how some chaotic chemists describe their discoveries. Test them out on your science teacher.

"No great discovery is ever made without a bold guess."

Sir Isaac Newton (1642-1727) discoverer of gravity and big fan of alchemy.

"Failure is the mother of success."

Hideki Yukawa (1907-1981) who discovered what some of the tiny bits of atoms are made of.

"The most important of my discoveries have been suggested by my failures."

Sir Humphry Davy (1778-1829) discoverer of many new chemicals.

Many surprising substances all owe their discovery to happy accidents.

FOUR DODGY DISCOVERIES

1 *Teflon*, the stuff used to coat non-stick pans, was only used for this purpose after 1955 because the inventor's wife was a bad cook. She kept getting her food stuck to the bottom of the saucepan.

2 *Vulcanized rubber*. Early rubber boots melted in hot weather. But in 1839 Charles Goodyear spilt some boiling rubber and sulphur. He found that the resulting sticky mess didn't melt so easily.

3 *Tracing paper* was invented by mistake in the 1930s because a worker at a paper factory put too much starch in a vat of wood pulp. The result was a strong but see-through paper.

4 *Silly Putty*, the bouncy modelling clay, was discovered in 1943 when scientists attempted to make artificial rubber from silicon. The substance was no good for tyres but the chemists had a lot of fun playing with it. A sharp-eyed salesman spotted the opportunity to develop a new toy and sold 250,000 Silly Putty balls in three days.

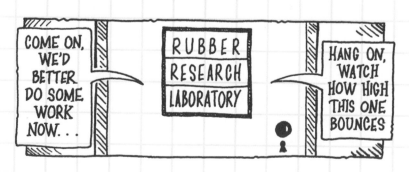

REVOLTING ROBOT RALLY

Once upon a time robots were dumb heaps of metal that only did one or two boring jobs. But that was then and this is now – and right now robots are getting smart and mean. We've organized a revolting rally for real-life robots ...

1 HITCH-BOT

In 2014 this brave little robot hitchhiked across Canada – on its own! Built by scientists at McMaster University, Ontario – the robot rover was a test to see how humans would react. In fact the robot made the trip and became a hero. Pity about those embarrassing yellow wellies and rubber gloves like your granny wears.

REVOLTING RATING

A NICE NOUGHT – this robot isn't revolting at all. It was so popular on the Internet that everyone offered it a lift.

2 ROBO-TEACHER

In 2014 a robot teacher named Nao made by Aldebaran Robotics taught kids at a Birmingham school. The 60 cm robot asked the kids questions and emailed their work to their parents. Several countries have plans for robo-teachers to help out human teachers.

REVOLTING RATING

AN OK ONE – you're not scared of a 60 cm-tall teacher are you? It doesn't even lose its temper when you give the wrong answer! Mind you, a mad scientist might build a giant robo-teacher with red eyes and steam coming out of its ears!

3 HUMAN-BOT

Japanese scientist Hiroshi Ishiguro wants to build a robot you could mistake for a human. He's already built a robot copy of himself and his robots are getting even more realistic – complete with silicone skin.

REVOLTING RATING

A TROUBLING TWO – fancy having a robot double? Your robot double could go to school, tidy your room and get the blame when you're naughty! Mind you, if its face fell off people would see it had eyeballs and false teeth stuck on a ball of metal bits. I bet they could tell the difference then!

4 NUKE-BOT

In 2011 Fukushima nuclear power station in Japan suffered a meltdown. Now it's full of deadly radiation and robots are tackling the clean-up. Each robot has job to do. Some clear rubble and others sweep the floor. There are even swimming robots and mopping robots.

REVOLTING RATING

A TERRIBLE THREE – it's a tough job even for a robot. One robot "died" when its optical fibre communication cord broke.

48

5 GUT-BOT

Imagine you're in space and you need a gut operation. BIG PROBLEM – there's no doc for millions of miles! Well, you need a robot surgeon developed by the Virtual Incision Company. The small robot burrows into your guts and fills them with gas and then operates from the inside.

REVOLTING RATING

A FEARSOME FOUR – space ops are scary because everything is weightless. Even your blood would float around in balls and splat on the walls. So would you want this scaled-down slice and dicer loose in your innards?

6 SNIFFY-BOTS

In 2013 Japanese scientists built two robots. One detects bad breath and the other – a robot dog – sniffs your socks. If you have bad breath, the bad breath robot says "NO WAY I CAN'T STAND IT!" If you have stinky socks, the robot dog growls and barks. Then it faints.

REVOLTING RATING

A FOUL FIVE – what rude robots! What's more the bad breath robot looks like a scary chopped-off head.

7 ROBO-RAT

In 2013 scientists at Waseda University, Tokyo wanted to make rats feel depressed so that they could test drugs to cheer them up. They built a robot rat bully to bump and chase the rats around and make them miserable.

REVOLTING RATING

A SINISTER SIX – even rats have feelings! I mean just imagine we built a robot-scientist bully to stress the scientists!

8 SEWER-BOT

Would you want to inspect a sewer? Me neither – that's why US firms RedZone Robotics builds robots to do the job. They've got cameras to make foul films of stinky sewers and sensors for hydrogen sulphide. Germs make this poisonous gas from rotting poo. The gruesome gas adds a rotten egg whiff to some farts.

REVOLTING RATING

A SICKENING SEVEN – the robots need humans to put them down the sewers and rescue them afterwards. Oh yes, and clean the poo off them!

9 ROBO-ROACH

Ever wanted a pet cyborg cockroach? It's sure to liven up your science lessons, especially when you make it run around to terrify your teacher! In 2013 US firm Backyard Brains made a kit that turned a cockroach into a remote-control robot cockroach. You control where it goes.

REVOLTING RATING

AN EVIL EIGHT – this kit is cruel! First you dunk the poor cockroach in freezing water to slow it down. You stick a tiny electric pack on its back and replace its antennae (feelers) with wires. Trouble is the cockroach learns to ignore your instructions (until it forgets to ignore them). And where will this end? Remote-controlled little sisters? Now that would be scary!

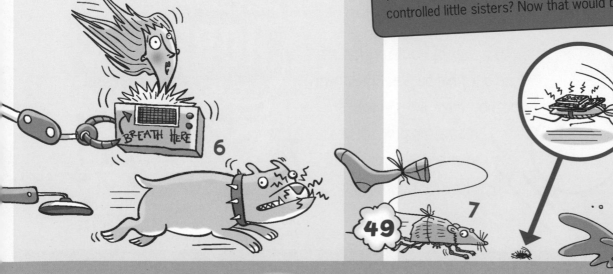

HORRIBLE SCIENCE
KILLER COMPETITION

If you want to win a host of *Horrible Science* goodies, now's your chance. Three lucky readers will each win ...

One *Horrible Science* Explosive Experiments kit. This is extremely explosive stuff! Create and launch a cool rocket, watch a volcano erupt, make a lava lamp and mix up some seriously slimy snot. Includes a 32-page Top Secret Lab Notebook. Age: from 10 years

One *Horrible Science* Smashing Solar System jigsaw puzzle.

A fabulous 300-piece jigsaw with horrible scenes of the Solar System and Oddblob the alien. Includes an 8-page Loony Leaflet stuffed full of foul facts. Science with the squishy bits in pieces! Age: from 8 years

For further information visit **www.galttoys.com** **GALT.**

PLUS a copy of *House of Horrors*. Find out what bugs eat their own poo, how many litres of wee a mouse can produce in a year and why you would hire a giant centipede.

To be in with a chance of winning, simply send us a drawing of your own original **robot creation**. Don't forget to give it a name, and label it to tell us exactly what it does. Maybe it's a robot that ties your shoelaces for you when you're late for school or a robot that does your homework for you! Or how about an awesome robot pet? Be as creative as you can.

Send your entry to:
Horrible Science Annual 2016 Competition
Scholastic Children's Books
Euston House
24 Eversholt Street
London
NW1 1DB

Don't forget to add your name, age, address and postcode to the back of the entry, so that we know where to send the prizes. Please get a parent or guardian to sign the back of your entry before you put it into an envelope.

The competition closes on 11th April 2016, and winning entrants will be notified within 28 days of the closing date.

THE BIG QUIZ

The amazing universe quiz

Here are some amazing universe facts which no teacher in the Solar System will know. Which facts are just too amazing to be true? Answer TRUE or FALSE.

1 When scientists discovered heat energy from the Big Bang – the huge explosion that happened at the beginning of time when the universe started to expand – they thought it was made by aliens.

2 Our galaxy contains millions of diamonds floating around in space.

3 Formalin has been found in space. (This is true, but what about the next bit?) On Earth this chemical is found in school dinners.

4 Astronomers have discovered alcohol floating around in space.

5 All the gold on Earth was made in exploding stars long before the Solar System formed.

Dinosaur-name quiz

Dinosaur names are often long and complicated and hard to pronounce. Oh, so you've noticed? Well, this quiz will help you handle the names in less time than it takes to say...

MICROPACHYCEPHALOSAURUS
(MY-CRO-PACK-Y-SEF-FA-LO-SORE-RUS

Dinosaur names are mainly in Latin and Greek and here's a handy guide to some of the words...

BARO = HEAVY
KENTRO = SPIKE
CEPHALO = HEAD
DINO = TERRIBLE
DONTO = TEETH
GASTRO = STOMACH

TYRANNO = TYRANT
SAUR/SAURUS = LIZARD
RHINO = NOSE
PACHY = THICK
HADRO = BIG
TRI = THREE
POD = FOOT
MICRO = SMALL

And here are some made-up dinosaur names. Now these dinosaurs really honestly don't exist, but as with many real names, the words used *describe* the dinosaur...

1 Hadropachycephalosaurus

2 Hadrodinodontosaurus

3 Barogastrosaurus

4 Microrhinokentrosaurus

All you have to do is work out what their names mean and then work out which of the dinosaurs below is which...

a)

b)

c)

d)

Fearsome fossils

This is a "have a go quiz". There are two possible answers so you've always got a 50 per cent chance of getting the right one.

I What was stolen by thieves in 1996?

a) A Tyrannosaur egg. The thieves planned to hatch out the dinosaur.

b) The world's only set of Stegosaurus footprints (set in solid rock).

2 Which of these creatures were around at the same time as the dinosaurs?

a) Frogs

b) Bats

3 Why did Dr William Hammer, discoverer of Crylophosaurus (cry-loaf-o-sore-rus), call his dinosaur skeleton "Elvisaurus"?

a) Because the dinosaur had a loud voice like megastar pop singer Elvis Presley (1935–1977).

b) Because the skull had a "hair-style" like Elvis.

"ROCK" STAR, JURASSIC PERIOD

ROCK STAR, SIXTIES PERIOD

4 The gingko tree was eaten by dinosaurs and thought to have died out. Where was a living gingko found?

a) In the garden of a Chinese temple.

b) On a remote island near the Arctic Circle.

5 The Carnegie Museum of Natural History in the USA had a complete Apatosaurus skeleton minus the head. What did they do?

a) Put the skeleton on display minus its head.

b) Put it on display with another dinosaur's head attached.

6 Fossils are bones, right? And bones are fairly light otherwise you wouldn't be able to lift your body out of bed in the morning. (Yes, it is possible.) So how come fossil bones need to be held up with steel rods?

a) Because fossil bones are made of solid rock.

b) Because dinosaur bones were heavier than human bones.

7 What are Black Beauty and Sue?

a) Horses hired for a dinosaur-hunting expedition.

b) Tyrannosaur skeletons.

8 What does the US company Dino Drops sell?

a) Jewellery made of lumps of dinosaur poo.

b) Dinosaur-shaped sweeties.

9 What can you do if you get cold on Axel Heiberg Island?

a) Burn a few fossils.

b) Shelter inside a dinosaur skull shaped like a cave.

10 What the heck was Hallucinogenia (ha-loo-sin-o-ge-nee-a)?

a) A type of winged dinosaur.

b) A type of prehistoric creature with seven pairs of legs and nozzles at each end and spikes on its back.

Spot that substance!

Here's a collection of chemicals. All you need to do is work out which question each one appears in.

Substances

a) DIAMOND

b) OZONE GAS

c) IRON PYRITE

d) VANILLALDEHYDE

e) GOLD

f) METHYL MERCAPTAN (ME-THILE MARE-CAP-TAN)

g) SOOT

1 This substance is so easy to roll flat that you could melt a lump the size of a matchbox and use it to cover a tennis court.

2 In this substance you'll find bucky onions and bucky bunnies. These are balls of carbon atoms and (believe it or not) bucky onions actually have layers like onions and bucky bunnies have "ears" like rabbits! Finding them must have been a hare-raising discovery.

3 In 1905 British King Edward VII was given a present of this substance and said:

I SHOULD HAVE KICKED IT ASIDE AS A LUMP OF GLASS HAD I SEEN IT UPON THE ROAD.

4 German chemist Christian Schönbein (1799–1868) discovered this substance after he noticed a nasty smell in his laboratory.

5 In 1578 explorer Martin Frobisher (1535–1594) risked his life to bring back this substance from the north of Canada thinking it was gold – it wasn't.

THIS GOLD IS LIKE SEAWATER

WHAT DO YOU MEAN?

THERE'S GALLEONS OF IT ALL AROUND US!

6 Just a pinch of this substance can pong out an entire sports stadium. (Clue: The chemical is also found in the flavouring of certain ice creams.)

7 The human body makes this substance from chemicals in asparagus and it makes the pee really whiffy. In the Second World War US pilots were given asparagus soup to eat if they were shot down. The pilots were told to pee in the sea and catch fish attracted by the smell.

YOU'RE KIDDING!

ANSWERS

Comet Get It!
pages 18–19

1 b) An Ariane rocket to be exact. You can't fly Rosetta like a plane because it doesn't have proper wings.

2 b) It can't be a) because you can't power any lamp.

3 a) It's all you can do. The astronauts are millions of km away!

4 a) You're a scientist – it's worth the risk to peek at Mars!

5 b) I said you're a scientist – you don't believe aliens have ever visited our Solar System. Studying the minerals that make up asteroids can tell you about how the Solar System was formed.

6 b) It's a great way to speed up the space probe and put it on the right course for the comet.

7 b) The comet has been somersaulting for millions of years. It won't stop anytime soon.

8 b) You can have half a mark for a) because the public were invited to name the landing site.

9 b) Philae is no bigger than a washing machine but it's packed with experiments to do on the comet. That's why it's there!

10 b) You've waited ten years already. What's a few months more?

Star-Struck Star-Spotter's Competition
pages 20–21

1 A1, G7

2 B7, C3, E7

3 A2, C4, D2, G1

4 F2

5 B10

6 A4, E10

7 C1, D10, E4, H9

8 D3

9 A3, E9, F4, F10, G3, G10 – there are three of each type

10 The band running from A5 to G6

11 C9

12 A6, E1, F8. The purple slobwobbler is in B2

Spot the Difference
pages 24–25

Dino Mayhem
pages 28–29

Odd Elements Quiz
page 36

1 Disgusting but TRUE. The alchemist was Hennig Brand (1630?-1692?, but nobody's really sure) and he made his discovery in 1669. It must have given him quite a shock - phosphorous glows in the dark.

2 TRUE. The place is called Ytterby and several elements were discovered there.

3 FALSE. It actually means "hard to get at".

4 TRUE. And unfortunately Berzelius died.

5 TRUE. In 1817 German chemist Friedrich Strohmeyer was analysing the chemicals in a bottle of medicine.

6 FALSE. But Krypton has been found floating around in space! The name means "secret" in Greek.

7 FALSE.

8 TRUE. It's the rarest of all the elements.

9 FALSE.

10 TRUE.

Spot the Lot
page 41

Quick Quesy Quiz
page 45

ALL the answers are b)!
1 b) Reindeer are more scared of polar bears than people. This may be because polar bears are more scary than people. The scientists' costume looked like an Egyptian mummy – so I guess they scared their mummies too.
2 b) Monkeys estimate and combine numbers but they can get the sums wrong. The scientists tested human students and they got the sums right.
3 b) The shock triggered memories in his brain.

THE BIG QUIZ
pages 52–55

The amazing universe quiz:
1 FALSE. The scientists working for the US Bell Laboratories in 1964 detected microwaves made by rapidly moving blips of heat energy given out by cooling gas after the Big Bang. But they thought the signals were interference caused by pigeon poo on their radar telescope and spent ages cleaning it before they realized that the pigeons were innocent.
2 TRUE. The Milky Way is full of diamonds. (That's our galaxy I'm talking about – not the choccie bar.) There's about one billion tonnes of diamonds just floating around up there – enough to make an entire planet! They're actually the remains of exploded stars.
3 FALSE. (Hopefully.) Formalin is used by undertakers to preserve dead bodies. It's poisonous – so you wouldn't want to taste it even if you fancied a "stiff" drink.
4 TRUE. There's enough alcohol in a typical chemical cloud in space to make 10,000,000,000,000,000,000, 000,000 (ten million billion billion) bottles of whisky.
5 TRUE. Gold is formed when stars explode.

Dinosaur-name quiz:
Answers: 1 c); 2 d); 3 b); 4 a); bonus: "Small thick-headed lizard". It's quite an insult so perhaps you could use it on the school bully. (Let's hope he doesn't understand Greek.)

Fearsome fossils:

1 b) The thieves cut them out of the solid rock.

2 a) Fossils prove that frogs lived in the time of dinosaurs. In fact, they appeared before most dinosaurs and of course they were around after the dinosaurs snuffed it.

3 b) The crest of the skull is shaped like Elvis's hair cut.

4 a)

5 b) It was a mistake because no one knew what an Apatosaurus skull looked like. It's unusual to find a complete dinosaur skeleton and most skeletons in museums are actually put together from the bones of several animals.

6 a) In a fossil the original material has been replaced by minerals. There's usually nothing of the original bone left.

7 b) Black Beauty's bones were blackened by a chemical called magnesium, and Sue got her name because she was found by a scientist named Sue.

8 a) They make cufflinks and tie-pins from fossilized dinosaur poo – quite the "dung thing" to wear.

9 a) And it does get a bit parky because the island is just 1,094 km (684 miles) from the North Pole. These fossils of 45-million-year-old trees on the island contain wood so well preserved that it actually burns. Of course, a true scientist would rather freeze than burn a fossil to keep warm.

10 b) It's probably the world's weirdest fossil. (NO, I don't care if your old fossil of a Science teacher is weirder. And no, you can't have a Hallucinogenia for a pet because they died out over 500 million years ago).

Spot that substance!

1 e) Actually, if you piled all the gold that has ever been found into a square block it could still fit inside that tennis court.

2 g) The first carbon balls to be found were buckyballs.

3 a) In 1905 Edward was given the world's largest diamond as a birthday present. Natural diamonds actually look like glass – it's only when they're cut that they really shine.

4 b) Ozone means "I smell" in Greek. The chemical, which normally takes the form of a gas, had been produced by a chemical reaction triggered by a powerful electrical current. And yes, this is the same gas that protects us from ultra-violet rays.

5 c) Iron pyrite is also known as "fool's gold". "I'm galled" as Martin might have said – but at least the pyrite made a useful road-building material.

6 d) The chemical is a concentrated form of vanilla flavouring.

7 f) The chemical is methyl mercaptan (me-thile mare-cap-tan) – said to be the most disgusting smell in the world. It reeks of rotten cabbage, garlic, onions, burnt toast and stinking blocked toilets. Fancy a sniff?

MiCROSCoPIC MONSTERS

Nick Arnold and
Tony De Saulles

NASTY NATURE

Nick Arnold and
Tony De Saulles

CHEMICAL CHAOS

Nick Arnold and
Tony De Saulles

Body Owner's HANDBOOK

Nick Arnold and
Tony De Saulles

DEADLY DISEASES

Nick Arnold and
Tony De Saulles

SPACE, STARS AND SLIMY ALIENS

Nick Arnold and
Tony De Saulles

SHOCKING ELECTRICITY

Nick Arnold and
Tony De Saulles

REALLY ROTTEN EXPERIMENTS

Nick Arnold and
Tony De Saulles

EVIL INVENTIONS

Nick Arnold and
Tony De Saulles